A Chinese Artist in
HARLEM

Ro

NATIONAL
GEOGRAPHIC
LEARNING

Australia · Brazil · Mexico · Singapore · United Kingdom · United States

Words to Know

This story is set in the U.S. It takes place in an area of New York City called Harlem, which is in the northern part of Manhattan Island.

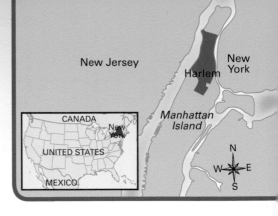

A **A Chinese Artist.** Read the paragraph. Then match each word or phrase with the correct definition.

The artist in this story, Mingliang Lu [mɪŋlæŋ lyu̱], paints beautiful landscapes, draws, and does calligraphy in the traditional Chinese style. He also paints flowers, animals, and lovely portraits of people. Ming was born in China, but now makes his living in New York City. He teaches children of various ethnicities—African-Americans, Latinos, Asians—about Chinese art and culture.

1. landscape _____	**a.** make money to live
2. calligraphy _____	**b.** a picture showing a view of the countryside
3. portrait _____	**c.** the race, culture, or nationality of a person
4. make a living _____	**d.** the art of creating fine, beautiful handwriting
5. ethnicity _____	**e.** a painting, photograph, or other picture of a person

a tiger

a portrait

an eagle

Chinese calligraphy

a landscape

B **Living in New York.** Read the paragraph. Then write each underlined word or phrase next to its definition.

Ming was born in the Chinese city of Shanghai [ʃæŋhaɪ], but now lives in the <u>cosmopolitan</u> city of New York. New York has many <u>immigrant</u> communities consisting of residents from around the world. Ming is helping the children of the city understand the importance of <u>diversity</u> and of accepting people from different backgrounds. <u>In the long run</u>, such work will hopefully increase understanding among people. In the immediate future, it may help to avoid <u>clashes</u> between different cultures in the city.

1. containing aspects from many parts of the world; international: _____
2. heated arguments or fights: _____
3. a person who has moved to another country to live: _____
4. continuing a long time into the future: _____
5. the inclusion of many different types of people or things in something: _____

With a population of approximately eight million, New York City is a huge cosmopolitan urban area. It is a **melting pot**[1] which consists of a large number of small neighborhoods that have **inhabitants**[2] from all over the world. These immigrant communities create a unique cultural mix that is exciting and different, and this cultural diversity has made New York famous.

The high cultural diversity of New York has both advantages and disadvantages, though. Sometimes, the differences between the cultures of the crowded neighborhoods result in conflict. Throughout the years, there have been a number of disagreements and even clashes between the different cultural groups in New York. However, many interesting and positive outcomes have also resulted from the **merging**[3] of backgrounds and traditions in the area. Artists in particular have often taken advantage of the opportunities that living close together has given them. They often use their cultural differences in order to learn from each other. One such artist, Mingliang Lu, has taken his skills to a neighborhood of New York called Harlem. Here, his goal is to enable others to learn about and understand Chinese art.

---

[1]**melting pot:** a place in which immigrants mix into the main culture
[2]**inhabitant:** a person who lives in a certain area
[3]**merge:** come together; join

🎧 CD 2, Track 01

并题记

Born in the Chinese coastal city of Shanghai, Ming has studied Chinese art for the majority of his life. At a very young age, he learned about calligraphy and painting from his father. He has never forgotten what he learned in his childhood, and has continued to paint and write even through some of the more difficult times in his life.

Ming moved from China to the United States in 1990, and today he lives in New York City where he continues to practice his art. He enjoys painting landscapes, flowers, animals, and even the symbol of the United States: the **eagle**.[4] Although he has been in the U.S. for a number of years, Ming's paintings are unmistakably Chinese; even the one of an eagle has a Chinese feel to it. Ming explains that as an immigrant to the U.S., he needed to use the skills he had acquired in his homeland to earn money in his new home. If he hadn't, he wouldn't have been able to survive. "When I first came to America," he explains, "my only skills were art. I didn't have other skills. I used my art to live, [I used it] to make a living."

---

[4]**eagle:** a large, strong bird found in the wilderness areas of North America and elsewhere

When he first arrived in the city, Ming set up his **easel**[5] on the streets of New York and drew and painted pictures of tourists in order to survive. Because New York is such a large, famous city that attracts many visitors, artists such as Ming are often able to make a living by painting portraits on the streets. They set up their painting equipment in popular tourist spots and then draw or paint portraits of people in order to sell them for money. But even for professional artists, it's not the easiest way to earn cash. In the winter, the streets can be freezing cold, in the summer they may get terribly hot, and the hours are always long. So, Ming eventually stopped painting on the street, and soon his professional life changed completely. He began to work for the New York Chinese Cultural Center.

---

[5]**easel:** a stand with three long legs and a narrow shelf in front used to hold a display or piece of art

Sequence the Events

What is the correct order of the events? Write numbers.

_____ Ming started to work for the Chinese Cultural Center.

_____ Ming left Shanghai.

_____ Ming painted portraits of tourists on the streets.

_____ Ming learned Chinese painting from his father.

_____ Ming came to New York.

Working for the New York Chinese Cultural Center enabled Ming to bring his artistic skills to the neighborhood of Harlem and allowed him to share his talents with the children of Public School 36. The neighborhood school was a place where Ming could use his painting skills to teach children about Chinese art and calligraphy. At the same time, he was given the opportunity to teach the children about Chinese culture as well. Now every day, instead of working on the streets painting pictures for visitors, Ming teaches children about his home country. It's a way of life that allows Ming to make an **invaluable**[6] contribution to the community, and it's a lifestyle that he obviously loves.

Amy Chin is the **executive director**[7] of the Chinese Cultural Center. In order to explain why she started the program, Chin refers to a well-known fact: very few artists can actually make a living as artists, and they must often take other jobs in order to survive. "As we all know," she says, "a lot of artists are not employed being artists. So I'm hoping that what we [can] do is to provide them [with] this opportunity." She then adds, "[We provide them with an opportunity] to really practice in the field that they've been trained for." Chin feels that teaching is an excellent opportunity for these artists to practice in the artistic field. They get to actually incorporate their training into their day-to-day jobs. For Ming, the idea seems to be working well and he's obviously happy about being able to use his skills. One can see how much he enjoys teaching while he shows the children how to draw and paint a tiger.

---

[6]**invaluable:** beyond value; very valuable
[7]**executive director:** the senior manager or business officer in a business or organization

Teaching at the public school, though, is about more than Ming and a way for him to make a living. The program benefits not only the artist, but the children as well. School principal Cynthia Mullen Simons says the program provides a wonderful incentive for her second-grade students to learn something new. She explains that the children are getting a chance to learn not only about different cultures and arts, but also about people and diversity. And the best part, according to Simons, is that they get to learn it **first hand**.[8] "You cannot teach **solely**[9] by the book, paper, and pencil," she states. "[The students] have to become involved. We need our students to hear, first hand, people from various cultures talk about their ethnicity. " In Simons' opinion, children need to understand that American culture is all a big melting pot.

In addition, 'learning by doing' is often thought to be an invaluable technique for teaching children. In order to facilitate this possibility, Ming often has the children paint with him in the classroom. As he presents information about art in the classroom, the children listen carefully. Then, after he creates a simple painting of a tiger in front of the class, he soon has one group of children busy making their own paintings. From time to time Ming stops to help each child get his or her painting just right. It's great fun for the students, and a wonderful opportunity to share knowledge across cultures.

---

[8]**first hand:** directly; by doing something oneself
[9]**solely:** just; only

The kids at the New York public school view Ming as their teacher from China, but Ming sees beyond ethnicity. He just sees students who really want to learn how to paint a simple tiger. In Ming's opinion, all children everywhere are just the same. "Chinese children, American children, Hispanic children, and black children," he says, "they are all the same." He then adds for emphasis, "[There's] no difference."

New York is already established as a diverse, international city, but even here programs like the Chinese Cultural Center's can still make a considerable difference. They can influence and alter the way children perceive people from different cultures as they grow up. They can also help to avoid cultural ignorance in younger generations. Chin explains, "When we bring these programs in, the kids get to see real people from another culture and to relate to them on many different levels." Simply working alongside people from different cultures helps children to better understand various types of people. It also helps them to become more accepting of diversity, which many people feel is essential for the welfare of society.

At Public School 36, school principal Cynthia Mullen Simons also talks about diversity and the educational importance of Ming's program. She suggests that it's actually the differences between human beings that make life so interesting. She also points out that for her, learning to understand these differences is an important educational aspect for the children. "What we don't want to do to our students is to make them ignorant to others and what others can bring," she says. "Our students need to understand that we are all human beings, that we all have different backgrounds ... different experiences ... and that's what makes us so interesting."

Fact or Opinion?

Read page 16 again and look at the following statements. Write 'F' for those statements that are factual, and 'O' for those that are an opinion.

1. Cynthia Mullen Simons is the principal of Public School 36. _____

2. It's the differences between human beings that make life interesting. _____

3. Learning to understand differences is an important educational aspect for children. _____

4. Simons does not want to make the school's students ignorant of others. _____

These days, in addition to being an artist, Ming is also serving as a kind of cultural **ambassador**[10] for his country. His role is to teach the children about China; its geography, culture, and civilization. More importantly, it's his job to teach them about the people of his country and to represent China to the children of Public School 36. In the long run, Ming's art may open the door to a whole different world for these children, and **broaden their horizons**.[11] He explains in his own words, "I feel like I am doing very important work." He then adds, "And it makes me really happy to teach calligraphy and painting to the children. I am introducing them to a wider world of Chinese culture. [I'm] giving them a greater understanding of Chinese people in the world and broadening their horizons."

As one watches Ming in the classroom, it becomes very clear that he is not only good in his role as a teacher, he is also excellent in his role of cultural ambassador. In Harlem, this Chinese artist has finally found a job that makes more than just a living; it makes a difference.

---

[10]**ambassador:** a government member that officially represents his or her country in another country
[11]**broaden (one's) horizons:** become more aware of or better understand something

After You Read

1. Why are there sometimes fights between people in New York?
   A. because their neighborhoods are too small
   B. because their cultures are different
   C. because they don't know each other well
   D. because there are too many people in New York

2. The writer suggests that Ming is:
   A. not close with his father
   B. nervous in New York
   C. proud of Chinese culture
   D. not a good artist

3. Which is NOT something that Ming paints?
   A. animals
   B. flags
   C. flowers
   D. landscapes

4. Ming could not find _____ easy way to make money as an artist.
   A. the
   B. an
   C. every
   D. no

5. Why did Ming find Public School 36 to be a place where he could use his painting skills?
   A. He was painting pictures on the school's walls.
   B. He could share his culture by teaching art.
   C. He was a good friend of the school's art teacher.
   D. The school was for Chinese students only.

6. The Chinese Cultural Center's program:
   A. enables artists to work using their skills
   B. does not employ artists
   C. gives students a chance to become artists
   D. none of the above

7. The school's principal said the program is important to her students for all of these reasons EXCEPT:
  A. Action is a good way for them to learn.
  B. Meeting different people teaches them that the world is a melting pot.
  C. They must learn by more than book, paper, and pencil.
  D. They now know how to draw a tiger.

8. In paragraph 2 on page 12, the word 'facilitate' can be replaced by:
  A. delay
  B. assist
  C. prevent
  D. practice

9. In paragraph 1 on page 15, to whom or what is Ming referring when he says 'they are all the same'?
  A. all art programs at New York public schools
  B. all American children in every state
  C. all children of different ethnicities around the world
  D. all children of different ethnicities at Public School 36

10. According to her statement on page 16, Cynthia Mullen Simons believes that:
  A. Students must understand that people's differences are good.
  B. It is okay for students to be ignorant.
  C. Ming is a popular teacher.
  D. Chinese culture is difficult for students to understand.

11. Why is Ming more than an artist?
  A. He is a calligrapher, too.
  B. He introduces children to new things in the world.
  C. He is broadening his own horizons in New York.
  D. He works for the New York Chinese Cultural Center.

12. What does the writer probably think about Ming?
  A. He should only teach art.
  B. He is an excellent artist.
  C. He makes a positive impact on his students' lives.
  D. He doesn't make enough money to live well.

Daily Journal
2008

April 3

Well, here I am in Chengdu, China! After I joined the teaching exchange program, I was a little nervous about my year abroad, but this is a great opportunity. I've been assigned a job teaching English and American culture at a local school here. The program has also arranged for me to live with someone from the area, the Li family. I feel so welcome in their home and now I can experience typical Chinese life first hand.

April 6

I'm glad I have a couple of weeks to get used to things before I start teaching; things here are pretty different from back home! One of the sons in my host family, Xiaoping who is 14, has taught me a lot, though. We take long walks every day to help me familiarize myself with the town and its inhabitants. Yesterday we passed a man who was selling little red bags of what looked like nuts. Xiaoping told me they were traditional Chinese medicines. He said some people in the area use various plants to treat illnesses. For example, part of a local flower is used to treat coughs. Amazing!

April 12

Today was the wedding of the oldest daughter in my host family, Meiyu, to Zhifeng and I was invited to attend as a special guest. At about 10:00 in the morning, a car covered with red decorations arrived and Meiyu was carried out to it. Xiaoping explained that her feet must not touch the ground until she reached Zhifeng's house. The actual wedding ceremony was short and simple, but the wedding

Class Schedule

Time	Monday	Tuesday	Wednesday	Thursday	Friday
9:00-9:50	Beginning English	Teachers' Meeting	Beginning English	Teachers' Meeting	Beginning English
10:00-10:50	Chinese Lesson with Ms. Hong		Chinese Lesson with Ms. Hong		Chinese Lesson with Ms. Hong
11:00-11:50	Intermediate English	Intermediate English	Intermediate English	Intermediate English	Intermediate English
12:00-12:50	Lunch	Lunch	Lunch	Lunch	Lunch
1:00-1:50	Language Lab	Language Lab	Language Lab	Language Lab	Language Lab
2:00-2:50	Advanced English		Advanced English		Advanced English
3:00-3:50		American Culture		American Culture	

dinner was just the opposite as I have never seen so much food in my life! What a great day!

April 14

I just got my new schedule for school and it is going to be rough! I have to be there at 8:00 in the morning and sometimes I don't go home until 5:00 at night. Teaching is always a difficult way to make a living, nevertheless I think it's worth it. In my case, I'll really have a chance to serve as a cultural ambassador for my home country and I'm sure that I'll be able to broaden my students' horizons—as well as my own. This is going to be a wonderful year!

CD 2, Track 2

Word Count: 381
Time: _____

Vocabulary List

ambassador (19)
broaden (one's) horizons (19)
calligraphy (2, 7, 11, 19)
clash (3, 4)
cosmopolitan (3, 4)
diversity (3, 4, 12, 15, 16)
eagle (7)
easel (8)
ethnicity (2, 12, 15)
executive director (11)
first hand (12)
immigrant (3, 4, 7)
inhabitants (4)
in the long run (3, 19)
invaluable (11, 12)
landscape (2, 7)
make a living (2, 7, 8, 11, 12)
melting pot (4, 12)
merge (4)
portrait (2, 8, 9)
solely (12)